Contents

About the Author

Anja Townrow was born in The Hague, Holland, and grew up in a village in the Dutch Polderland. After studying English language and literature at the University of Leiden, she moved to England in 1974. Since the late 1980s when quilting magazines and books from the United States became more widely available in the United Kingdom, she has been greatly inspired by American quilters.

Anja is a self-taught quiltmaker who has won many prizes for her work. She travels extensively, teaching in Britain and Europe. Known for her use of vibrant colors, Anja's ever-expanding range of patterns is produced under the name of Dutch Quilts, and her designs can also be found as regular contributions in various patchwork publications.

For more information about Dutch Quilt patterns and quilts, visit Anja's website at www.anjatownrow.com.

General instructions

There are step-by-step foundation piecing instructions for those of you who are new to the technique. They are also a handy reference if you need to brush up on your skills. All this begins with an invaluable collection of tips for frustration-free foundation piecing.

But first…

A cautionary tale

Do you recognize this quilter? While on her twice-weekly pilgrimage to a favorite quilt shop, Avida Piecer spots a new book on the shelves. Attracted by the bright cover, she picks it up, leafs through it, and sees a picture of a quilt she simply must make.

Avida adds the book to her pile of fabrics and other impulse buys. Having stacked her haul on the passenger seat of the car so she can fondle her purchases while waiting at traffic lights, she rushes home. Once there, Avida starts on her new project straight away without bothering to read the general instructions in the book (she is, after all, quite an experienced quiltmaker and has a fair idea of the methods used to construct the design).

Very soon, Avida encounters a slight hitch. She ignores it and continues sewing, confident that she knows how to overcome this small problem.

Not long after, Avida finds herself in trouble, unable to complete the next step in the patchwork process. Then she has a bright idea and looks more closely at her new book, turning to that boring bit describing the techniques used to make the projects. It gradually becomes clear to her that she could have avoided a lot of frustration had she just allowed herself to read through the general instructions.

I know Avida well. I am Avida. We've all been there, done that, and have a half-finished quilt to show for it!

So even if you are familiar with foundation piecing, please read through the following pages to help avoid any problems you might encounter with some of the more complicated blocks.

Tips for happy patchworkers

Patchwork and quilting is a hobby and should therefore be enjoyable and relaxing. If you find yourself treating it as an unpleasant chore, take a step back and ask yourself how you can make it rewarding once again. You may simply need to give yourself time to learn a new technique, an effort that may be tricky initially, but will eventually give much satisfaction. You may need to invest in better tools, or organize your workspace so you are more comfortable.

If you are happy with what you are doing, it will show in your quilts! The following tips should help you toward frustration-free foundation piecing.

Mark color choice on the tracing

Marking the color on the tracing takes a lot of guesswork out of the process while sewing, thus cutting down on mistakes and the need to unpick. Pattern pieces are very irregular in shape and size, and it is not always easy to identify their position in the color picture once you have started piecing.

Don't worry about fabric grainlines

Stitching on subsequent patches will stabilize the pieces as you work. On long, straight pieces, you will automatically have the correct grain line, because you will have pre-cut a straight strip.

Handle with care!

Once the paper has been removed, vulnerable bias edges will be exposed, so it is important not to distort the seam allowances by pulling or pressing. Press when the blocks are completely assembled.

Use neutral thread

Removing the freezer paper can be quite hard on stitching, so make sure that your stitches won't show. Light colored thread tends to show up more than a neutral khaki or beige.

Use pieces of a generous size

The most common problem in foundation piecing seems to be an overly-careful attitude some quilters have toward cutting up their fabric. Trying to position too-small pieces of fabric takes a lot of time and often leads to unpicking in the end. Find a happy medium between wasting material and wasting time.

Use a large stitch to baste the patch

When in doubt, select a bigger piece. Or try this trick: When unsure about whether a particular piece of fabric is large enough for the number to be covered, stitch the piece in place with a large basting stitch and press it over to check the fit.

If the patch doesn't quite cover the relevant number, the big stitches are easy enough to unpick, so that you can try again. If it does fit, stitch over the long stitches with a regular stitch, then trim and press as usual.

Unpicking

If you have to unpick, use a seam ripper to slash every third or fourth stitch on the fabric side of the work. Do not pull at the stitches on the paper side, as this will cause the paper to crumple and tear, and the drawn line will be lost. Once the stitches have been loosened on the fabric side, pull and remove the ends of those stitches. Then turn to the stitching on the paper side, and you will find that the entire line of stitching can easily be removed by pulling at the ends of the thread.

Trimming seams

Use an Add-A-Quarter™ ruler, rotary-cutter, and a thin straight-edge, such as a card, to trim the seams. Place the card on the seam line and fold back the foundation paper along the card's edge. Place the Add-A-Quarter™ ruler along the folded paper edge and trim the excess fabric from the seam using the rotary-cutter.

After sewing a light patch onto a dark patch, you may note that the edge of the underlying dark seam is still visible after trimming the seam. In that case, peel the light-colored seam back and shave an extra sliver off the edge of the dark seam. It is well worth doing this to enhance the look of your finished quilt. There is nothing as ugly as a dark seam showing through the front of the quilt, something usually not noticed until the work is hanging on a wall.

Trouble-free triangles

A row of triangles in a pattern can present unique cutting and sewing challenges. To avoid frustration, do yourself a big favor and make a pre-cutting template. Simply trace one of the largest triangles in the row onto a piece of paper. Cut out the shape, adding roughly ½" around all traced lines. Use this shape to pre-cut all the triangles in the row.

General instructions

If the triangles form an arc, the triangles on the outside edge of the arc are larger. To accommodate the different sizes, make separate templates for triangles on the outer and inner edges.

Positioning a motif or striped fabric

Whenever you want a fabric to go onto a particular spot in the tracing, identify the middle of that area with a pencil mark. Stick a pin through the middle of the fabric motif from the wrong side and then stick the pin through the paper at the pencil mark. Pin along the rest of the drawn line and use a basting stitch to secure the piece. When satisfied with the position of the fabric, stitch it in place.

The method

The technique used to construct the patchwork in this book may be quite different from your methods.

The patterns are designed and drawn as one block, then the block is divided into template sections for foundation piecing, and single-piece templates.

The design is treated as a jig-saw puzzle, where the separate paper templates are re-assembled in fabric form. To do this accurately, a seam line is drawn on all fabric pieces with the help of the freezer paper templates. Marks are added to the seam lines where they can help in construction and eliminate confusion.

Making freezer paper templates

In this book, where the patterns are too large to be printed on one page, they have been split. Make a master tracing of the entire pattern piece on plain paper. Match up the pieces at the broken line indicating where the pieces should be joined. It is advisable to have this master pattern so you can make any subsequent tracings

easily and accurately. In the case of the THISTLE POT pattern, the flower part (Section A) is printed in four sections. Line up the pattern pieces at the broken lines to make a master tracing of the complete Template A pattern.

Trace the pattern pieces onto the dull side of freezer paper. Transfer all numbers and marks from the pattern. The marks at the edges of patterns will help you line up the pieces when you are ready to assemble the blocks. In some cases, you may find that the marks correspond to seam intersections on the next patch. Whenever you have the slightest doubt, always refer back to the main pattern drawing to find out exactly what fits where.

Reverse patterns are given in this book so you can trace them onto freezer paper without worrying about making a mirror image.

Cut the freezer paper templates exactly on the outside lines; fabric seam allowances will lie outside these lines.

Piecing the blocks

Identify the pattern pieces given for the block and make the freezer paper templates.

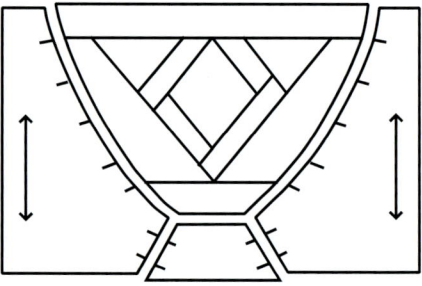

Identify pattern pieces and make templates.

Cut the freezer paper templates exactly on the solid outside lines. Do not cut the numbered templates apart, as these are to be kept whole for foundation piecing. Seam allowances are added outside of the lines in fabric form only, not on the freezer paper template. Transfer all marks and numbers from the paper tracing onto the freezer paper templates.

Indicate your color choices on the templates with the help of the list given in the block instructions. Remember that the templates show the block in mirror-image, so compare your fabrics to the color illustrations.

Foundation piecing

You will be sewing on the drawn lines on the dull side of the freezer paper. The fabric picture will appear right side up on the other side, with the wrong side of the fabric sticking to the shiny side of the freezer paper.

Locate #1 on the template. Select a piece of fabric large enough to cover the #1 area plus seam allowances. Iron or pin the wrong side of the fabric to the shiny side of the freezer paper.

Iron wrong side of fabric to shiny side of freezer paper.

Turn to the drawn side and hold the paper and fabric to a light source to check for adequate seam allowances beyond the lines of #1.

Re-position the fabric piece if necessary.

Find #2 on the freezer paper template. Select a piece of fabric large enough to cover #2 plus a generous seam allowance. Place the #2 fabric piece right sides together with the #1 fabric piece. Do not be tempted to align the raw edges of both patches; this has no relevance in this method since you do not have exact seam allowances but roughly cut patches.

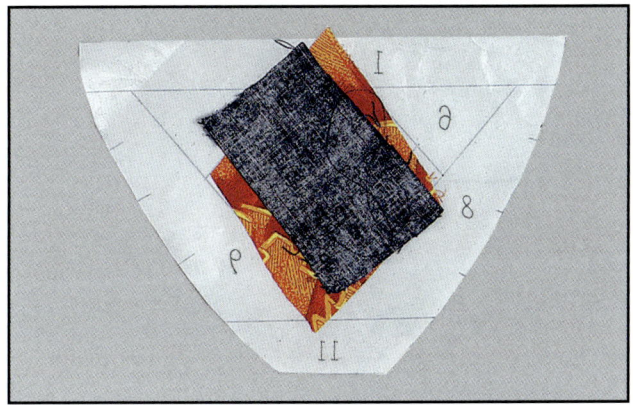

Position second piece right sides together with first.

If you have trouble finding the correct placement, create a mock-up of how the two patches will appear together in the block once they have been sewn. This will give you an angle on which way to turn fabric piece #2 to lie on piece #1.

Keep a white sheet of paper next to your sewing machine and use it as a background to help you position the fabric onto the undrawn side. You will find that you can peek through the freezer paper template and see the lines far more clearly with the help of the light background.

You will be sewing on the line between #1 and #2 on the drawn side of the template. Check that you have placed the fabric patch correctly to catch this line. Make sure also that the fabric will cover the entire area of #2 on the template after

General instructions

sewing and pressing over, with seam allowances beyond the drawn lines for the patch. Once you are happy about the placement, put in some pins to hold fabric and paper together.

Turn to the drawn side and sew on the line between areas #1 and #2 through all layers – paper and fabrics pieces #1 and #2.

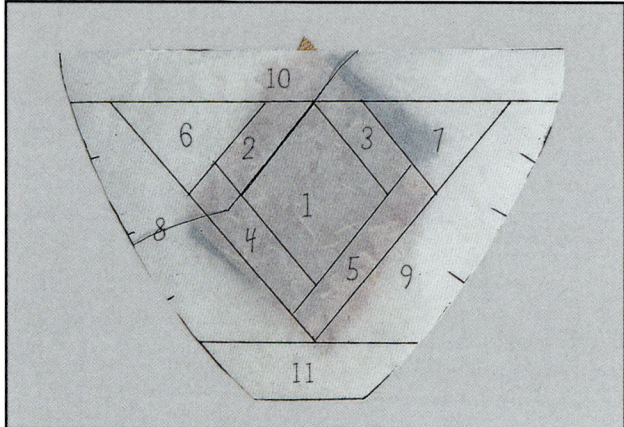

Sew on the line between #1 and #2.

Sew with a slightly shorter stitch than usual and start and finish four or five stitches beyond either end of the line. Trim the seam and press fabric piece #2 over the shiny paper patch #2.

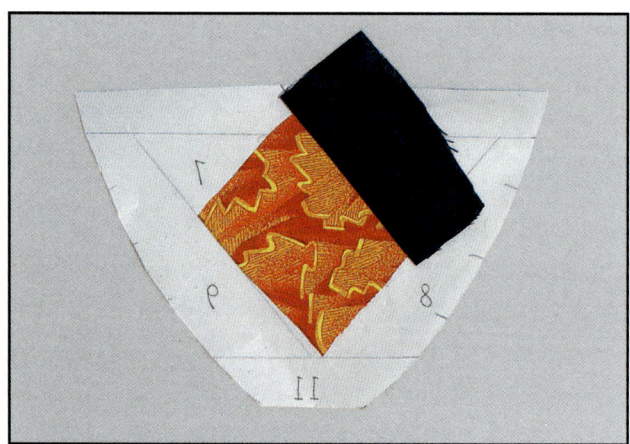

Press fabric #2 over shiny paper #2.

Continue with #3 and subsequent numbers in the same way.

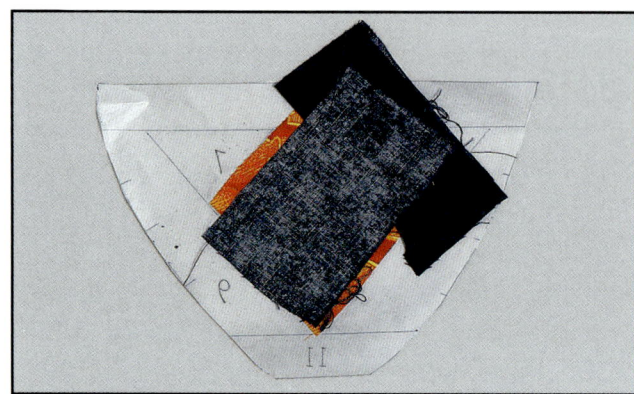

Continue adding fabric pieces in numerical order.

Identify the next sewing line by finding the next patch in numerical order. Then find the line that lies between that patch and the numbers already sewn; stitch on that line.

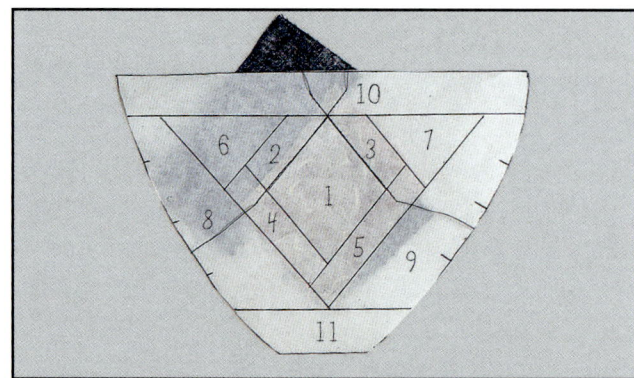

Stitch on lines between sequential numbers.

Make sure you leave a generous seam allowance around the outside edge of the template.

Leave a generous seam allowance.

You will become more confident with experience, and as long as you use fabric patches of generous size, you will soon settle into a steady piecing rhythm. Beware of any very irregular shapes on the tracing and make absolutely sure that your patches are large enough to cover any outward angles of the shape.

When you stitch the patches bordering the outside edge of the template, stitch well into the seam allowance, so you can be confident that those stitches won't unravel when you remove the paper at the end of the piecing sequence. I cannot count the number of times a little "remedial" work was necessary when this advice was not followed.

After piecing all the numbers, draw a seam line around the edge of the freezer paper on the wrong side of the fabric, transferring all the marks onto the fabric.

Remove the paper carefully. Begin at the outer edges by pinching the stitching in the fabric seam allowance firmly between finger and thumb and then working the paper loose. Using this method will lessen the chance of unraveling stitches. When the paper is removed, the completed section is ready to sew to the rest of the block.

After a foundation piecing session, remove the sewing machine needle you have used from your machine and put it in a separate holder. It will only be fit to use for your next foundation piecing project, since sewing through paper will have made it too blunt for normal use.

Selecting fabric

"Where do you get your fabrics?" or "How do you pick your colors?" are the questions I hear most often from fellow quilters.

I could offer a lengthy explanation, but the answer can really be given in one word: instinct. No matter how long I study books that contain in-depth analysis of the use of color, showing the color wheel and various charts, I never seem to be able to put any of my new knowledge into practice. Extensive reading on the subject has given me a grasp of some basic rules, but when it comes to choosing colors for my quilts, instinct takes over. As soon as I think about rules and theory, I get into trouble and become positively paralyzed, suddenly unable to put any two fabrics together.

So if your total theoretical knowledge of color amounts to the fact that blue and yellow make green, don't despair and don't feel you are "hopeless with color." Choosing fabrics and colors is just a matter of personal taste. Be confident of your color choices. If you like it, then use it.

Here are some useful fabric selection tips:

■ Choose a printed fabric that you really like and pick out the colors in the print for the rest of the fabrics in the quilt. To add interest, introduce a "surprise" color into the scheme.

■ Resist the tendency to over match fabrics. Adding a clashing, totally different fabric to a "matching" selection can add vibrancy to your Flower Pot blocks. Keep that in mind when selecting colors, and add the unexpected.

■ Try anything that catches your eye. As soon as you spot a fabric on the shelf that looks promising, put it with your other selections. Don't dismiss a strange, strongly-patterned fabric; instead, ask yourself how you can make it work for you. Perhaps you could cut a motif from it to appliqué onto a pot or into the center of a quilt to provide an interesting focal point for the piece.

■ Make small quilts at first, so it is not a disaster if you don't like them. They will still be a much appreciated present or donation to charity. Put it down to experience and move on to the next quilt with a better idea of how you want to use colors in your new project.

■ You could also choose your background fabric first. Many of the quilts in this book use strong, bright fabrics as backgrounds. That means that the rest of the colors have to be fairly powerful to stand out against the background.

■ Do your own thing and don't listen to prevailing "wisdom." For example, a few years ago, it became accepted as common knowledge among quilters that yellow is a difficult color to use. Is that based on fact, or rumor? Find out for yourself! Perhaps you'll find that yellow is not so difficult after all.

■ Consider stripes and border fabrics! These designs always work very hard to pay for their keep. In fact, many of the quilts pictured in this book rely heavily on striped fabric for their impact. When a striped design stands on its own in a pot or border, it also often allows the quilter to do less piecing. Stripes and border fabrics have worked so well for me that when I see a nice striped or border fabric, I purchase at least two yards of it to add to my collection.

■ When choosing fabrics for Flower Pot quilts, avoid using too much green in the pots, as you will then be struggling to find something suitable for the leaves. Pick an accent color for use in the pot that can be brought back into the flowerhead, thus creating a balance in the design.

THISTLE POT

Block Size 14½" x 25"

Since the curves that shape the pot are very gentle and easy to sew, this an excellent project for a first try at curved piecing. The block is made in two parts that combine foundation piecing with curved piecing: a foundation pieced flower part, Section A; and a pot part that includes Section B, C and pieces, D and Dr.

THISTLE POT

THISTLE POT

Color Selection

Section A

Piece	Color
2, 3, 6, 7, 10, 11, 14, 15, 18, 19, 20	Light Green
1 (4" x 3")	Yellow
4 (5" x 3")	Orange
5 (4" x 7")	Red
8 (6" x 3")	Deep purple
9 (8" x 4")	Fuchsia
12 (3" x 7")	Olive green
13 (10" x 4")	Medium green
16 (4" x 9")	Sage green
17 (9" x 4")	Dark green

Make a copy of pattern pieces by tracing or using a non-distorting photocopier. Join pattern sections on dashed lines as indicated. Make a full-sized master copy of the entire pattern before tracing pattern pieces onto the dull side of freezer paper.

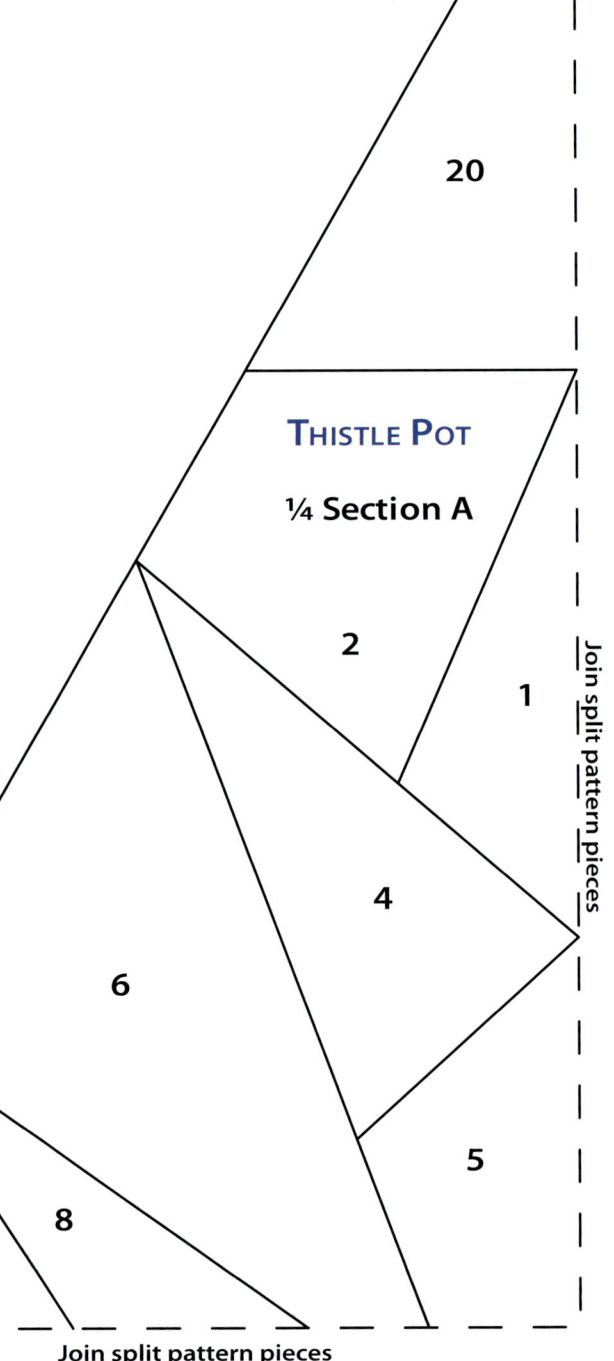

Add generous seam allowances (¼" to ½") to all fabric pieces when cutting.

THISTLE POT

¼ Section A

Join split pattern pieces

Join split pattern pieces

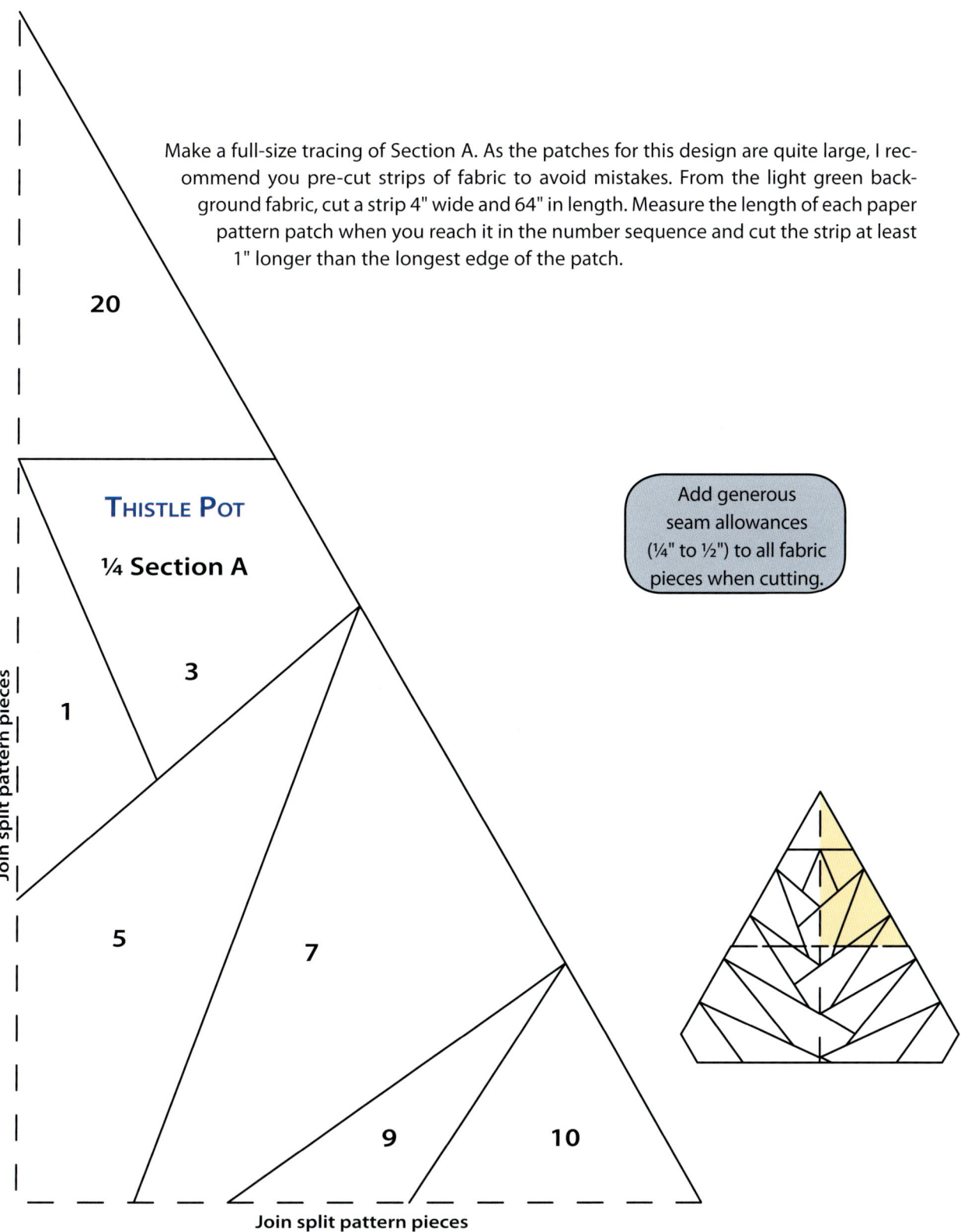

Make a full-size tracing of Section A. As the patches for this design are quite large, I recommend you pre-cut strips of fabric to avoid mistakes. From the light green background fabric, cut a strip 4" wide and 64" in length. Measure the length of each paper pattern patch when you reach it in the number sequence and cut the strip at least 1" longer than the longest edge of the patch.

THISTLE POT

¼ Section A

Join split pattern pieces

20

1

3

5

7

9

10

Add generous seam allowances (¼" to ½") to all fabric pieces when cutting.

Join split pattern pieces

THISTLE POT

Make a copy of pattern pieces by tracing or using a non-distorting photocopier. Join pattern sections on dashed lines as indicated. Make a full-sized master copy of the entire pattern before tracing pattern pieces onto the dull side of freezer paper.

Add generous seam allowances (¼" to ½") to all fabric pieces when cutting.

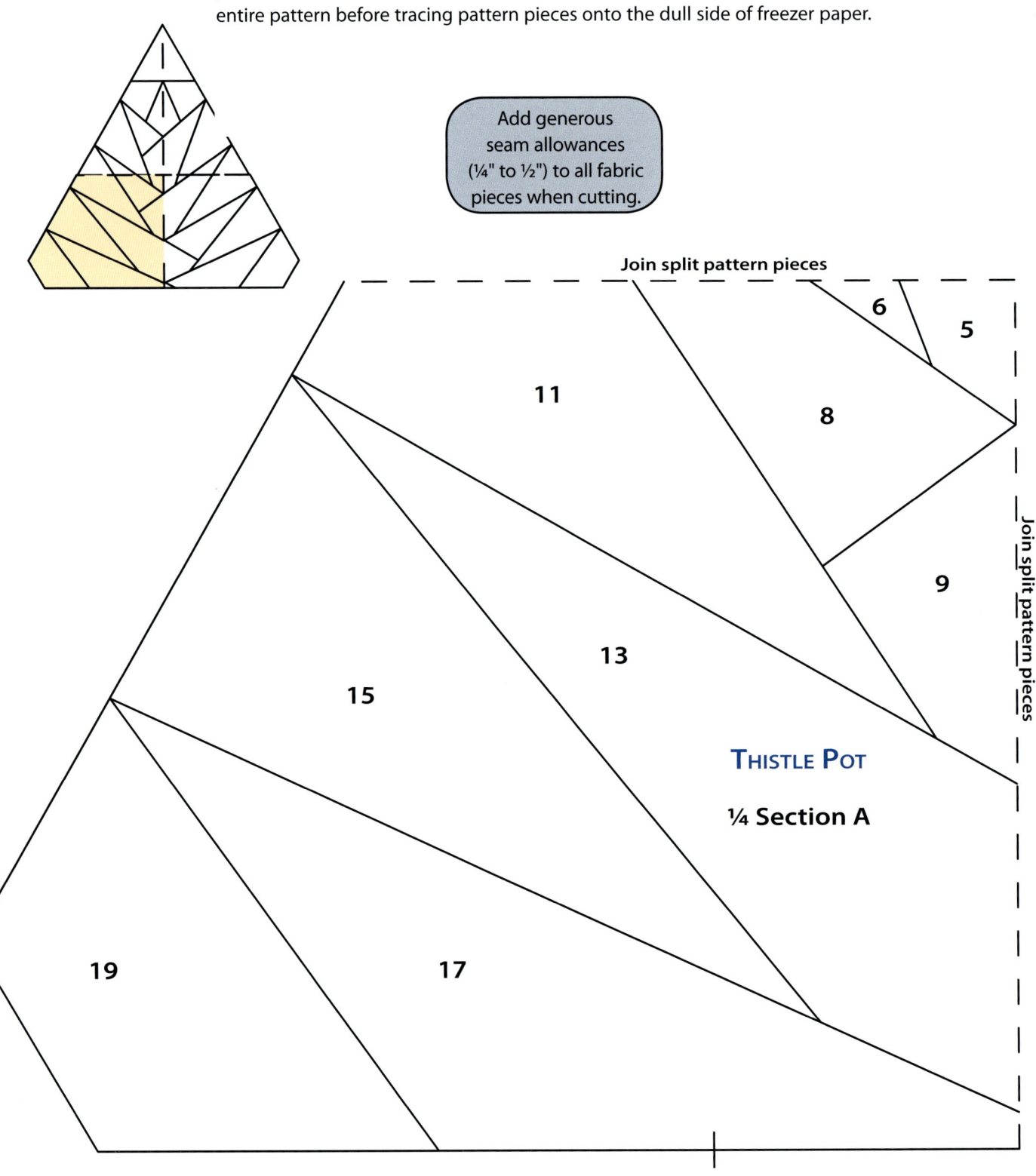

Join split pattern pieces

6

5

11

8

9

Join split pattern pieces

13

15

THISTLE POT

¼ Section A

19

17

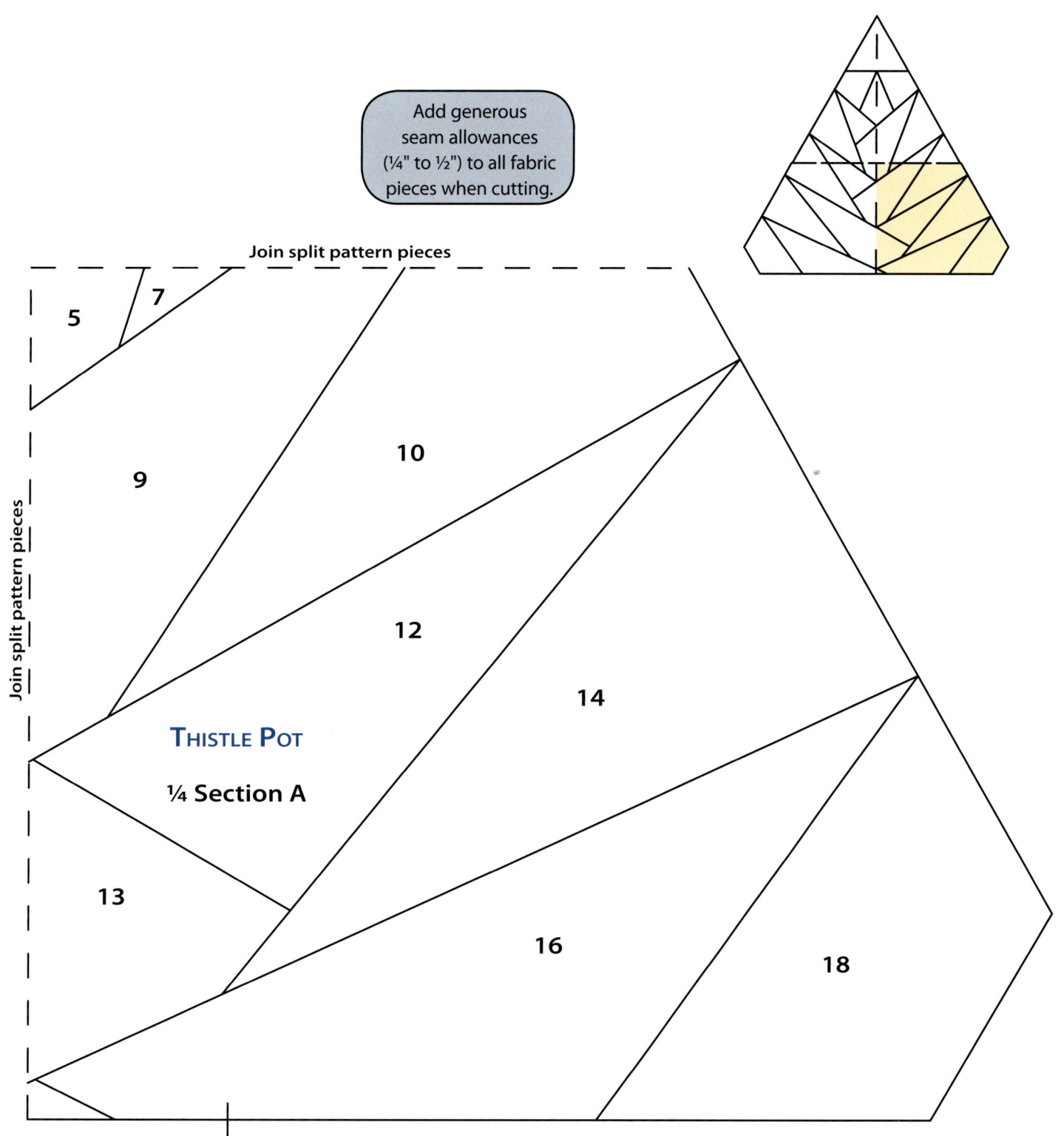

Add generous seam allowances (¼" to ½") to all fabric pieces when cutting.

Join split pattern pieces

Join split pattern pieces

5

7

9

10

12

14

THISTLE POT

¼ Section A

13

16

18

THISTLE POT

THISTLE POT
Color Selection
Section B

Piece	Color
1, 4, 5, 8, 9	Yellow
2, 3, 6, 7, 10, 11, 14, 16	Deep Purple
12, 13, 15	Red

Add generous seam allowances (¼" to ½") to all fabric pieces when cutting.

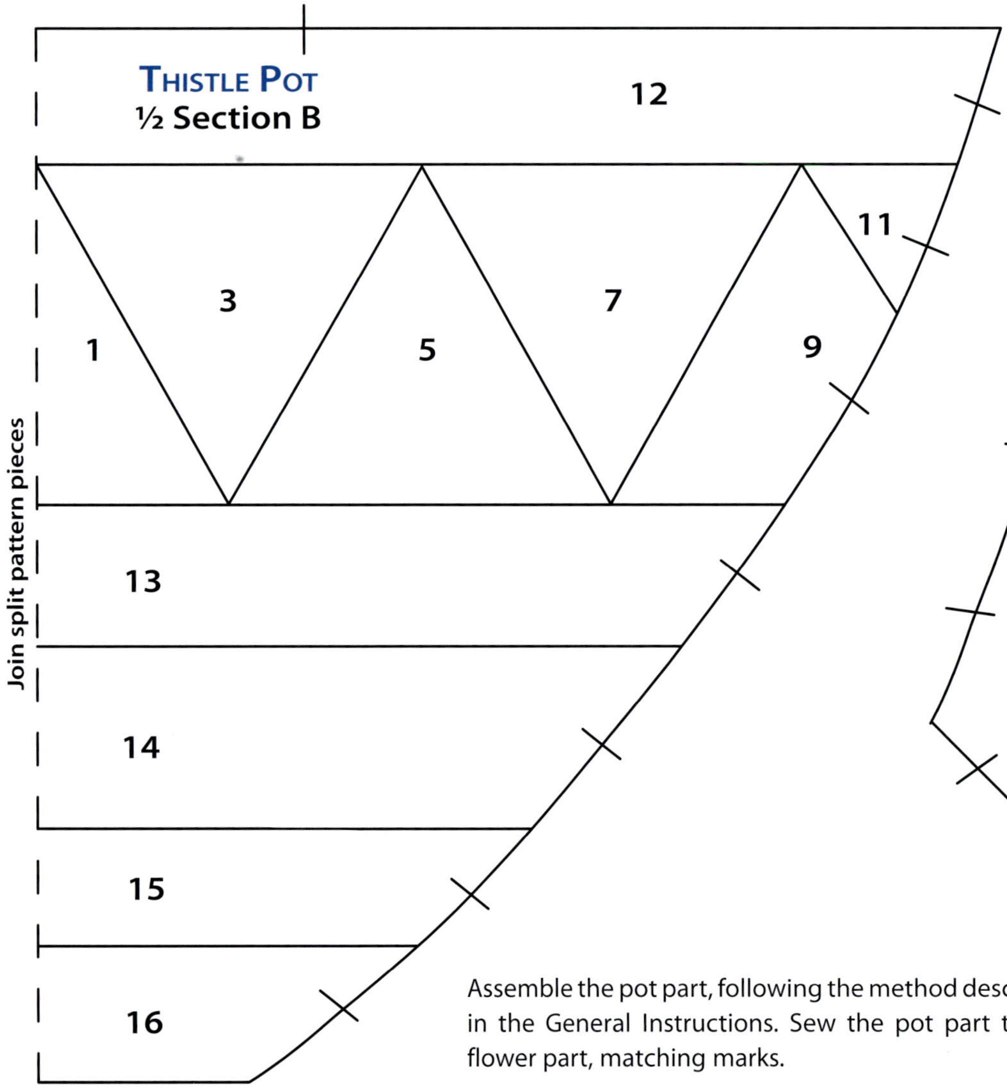

THISTLE POT
½ Section B

12

11

3

1

7

5

9

13

14

15

16

Join split pattern pieces

THISTLE POT
Piece Dr

Assemble the pot part, following the method described in the General Instructions. Sew the pot part to the flower part, matching marks.

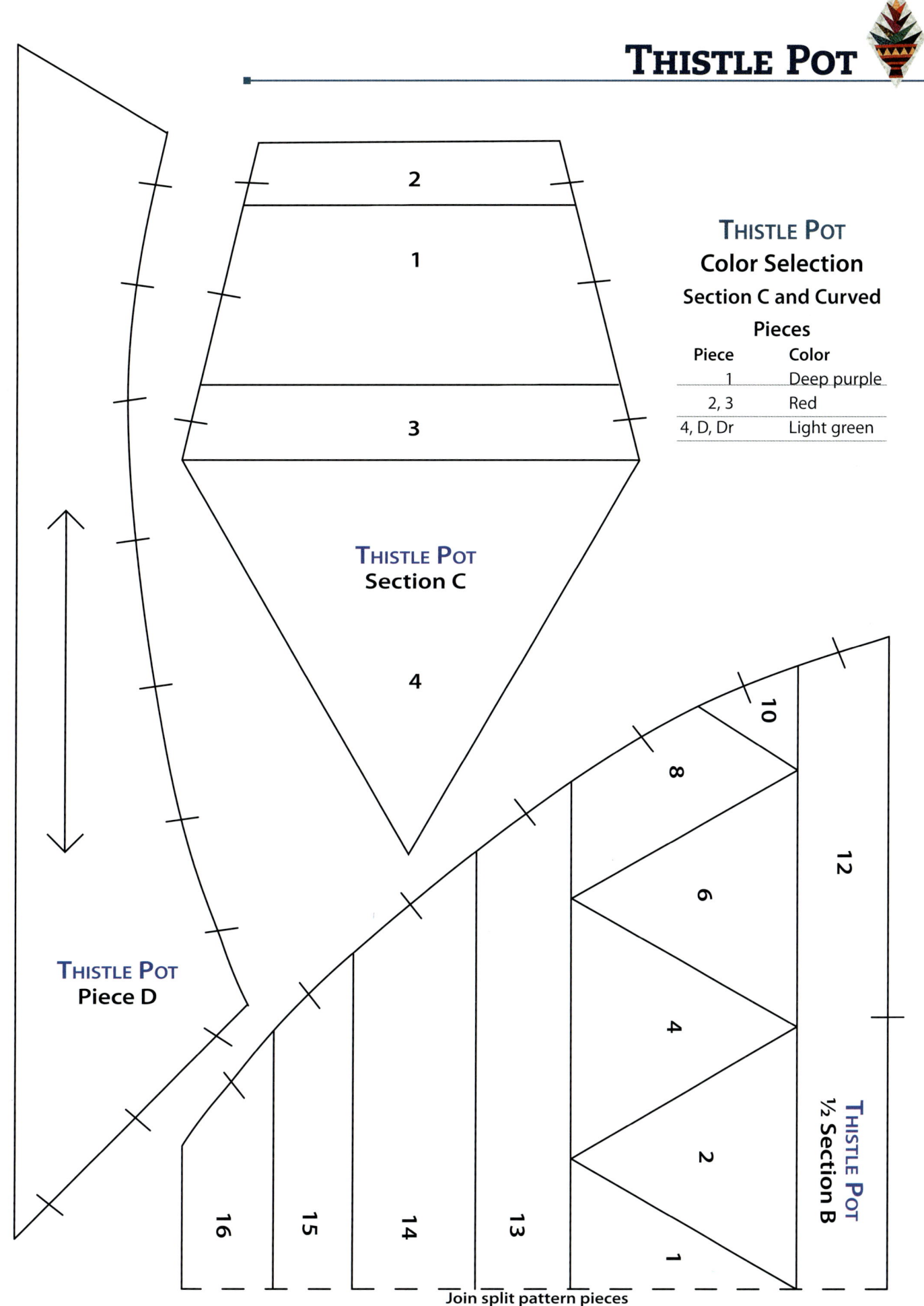

2

1

3

THISTLE POT
Color Selection
Section C and Curved
Pieces

Piece	Color
1	Deep purple
2, 3	Red
4, D, Dr	Light green

THISTLE POT
Section C

4

THISTLE POT
Piece D

10

8

12

6

4

2

THISTLE POT
½ Section B

16

15

14

13

1

Join split pattern pieces

THISTLE POT VARIATIONS

TRELLIS THISTLE
23½" x 34"
Careful color placement will result in the airy trellis effect.

PAINTED THISTLE
14½" x 25"

The blue/green corners pick up the blue from the pot and the green of the leaves. The quilting, done by Jackie Tonks in a wide variety of threads, stitches, and freehand techniques, makes this small quilt really special.

CACTUS POT

Block Size 8" x 8"

Simple foundation piecing combined with two gentle curves make this plump little flower pot a lovely addition to your block library.

The block is made in two parts: the flower part, Section A, and the pot part, Sections B, D, and pieces C and Cr.

> Add generous seam allowances (¼" to ½") to all fabric pieces when cutting.

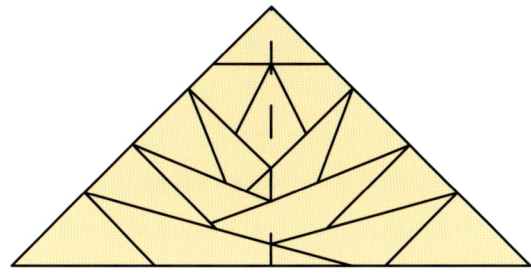

CACTUS POT
Color Selection
Section A

Piece	Color
2, 3, 6, 7, 10, 11, 14, 15, 16	Light Green
1	Pink
4	Red
5	Aubergine
8	Medium purple
29	Fuchsia
12	Bright green
13	Medium green

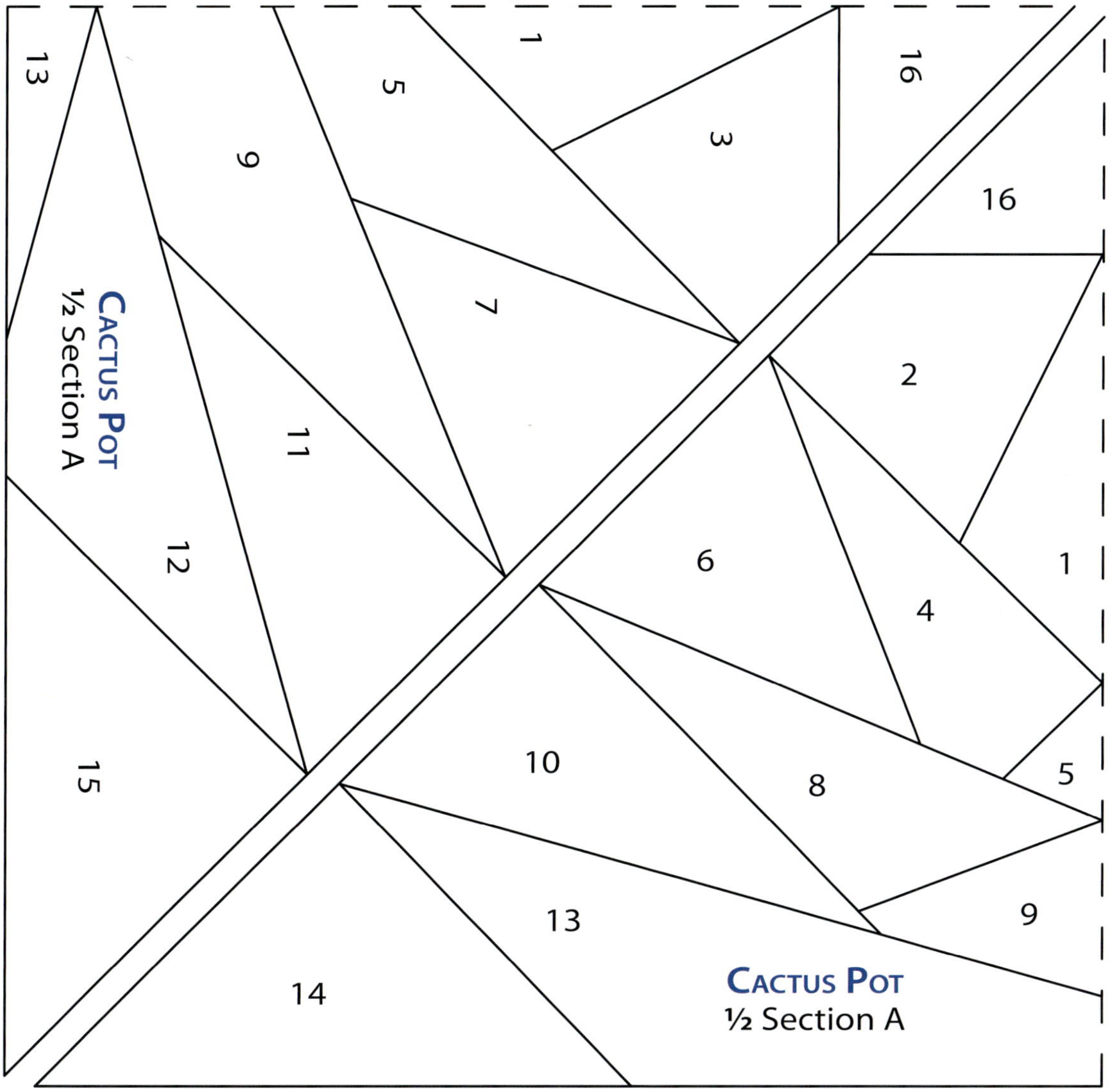

Join split pattern pieces

13 1 5 16 9 3 7 16 2 11 6 1 4 12 10 8 5 15 13 9 14

CACTUS POT
½ Section A

Join split pattern pieces

CACTUS POT
½ Section A

CACTUS POT

CACTUS POT
Color Selection
Section B

Piece	Color
1, 4, 5	Red
2, 3, 6, 7	Yellow
8, 9	Deep Purple
C, Cr	Light green

> Add generous seam allowances (¼" to ½") to all fabric pieces when cutting.

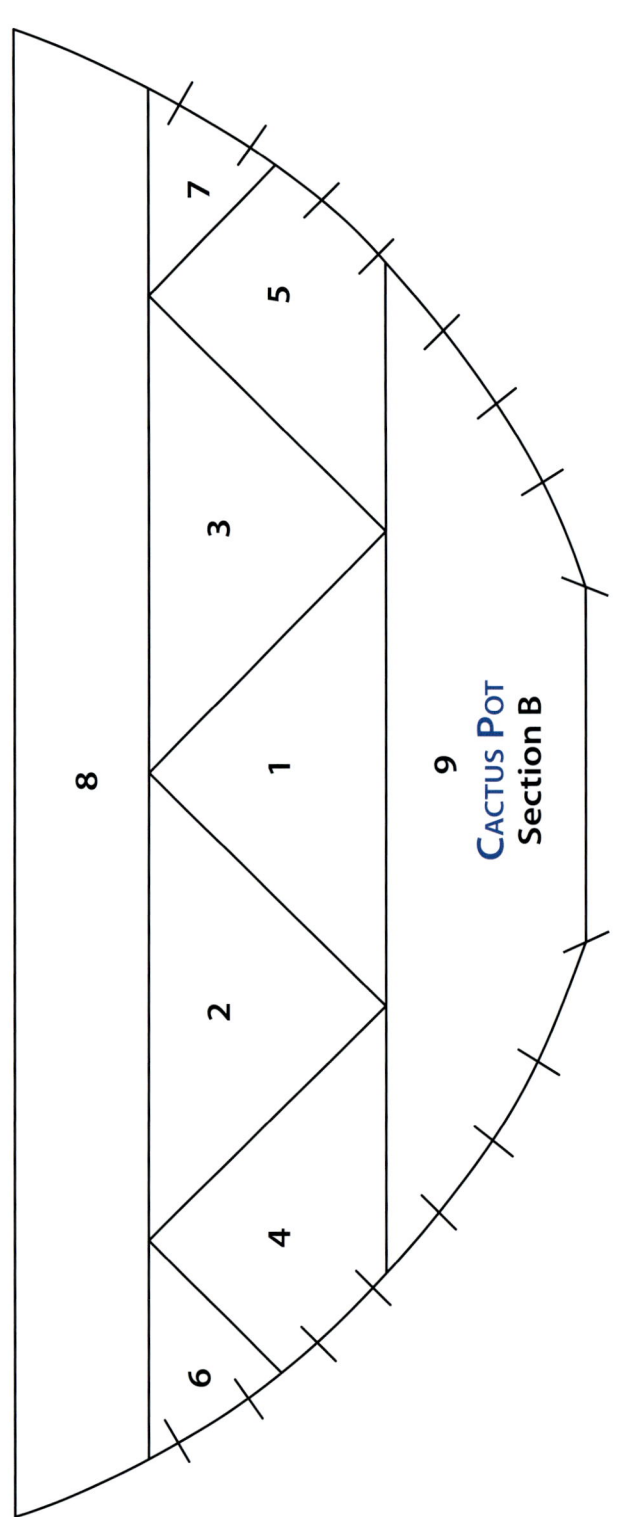

CACTUS POT
Section B

CACTUS POT
Color Selection
Section D

Piece	Color
1	Deep Purple
2	Light green

Foundation piece the sections, and assemble the pot part following the method described in the General Instructions. Join the flower section to the pot section.

> Add generous seam allowances (¼" to ½") to all fabric pieces when cutting.

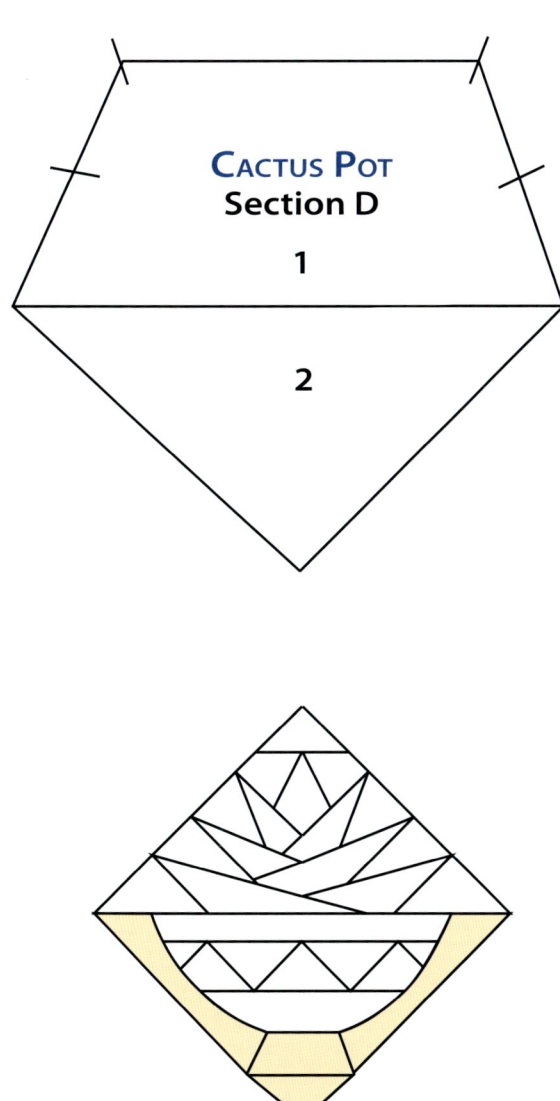

CACTUS POT
Section D

1

2

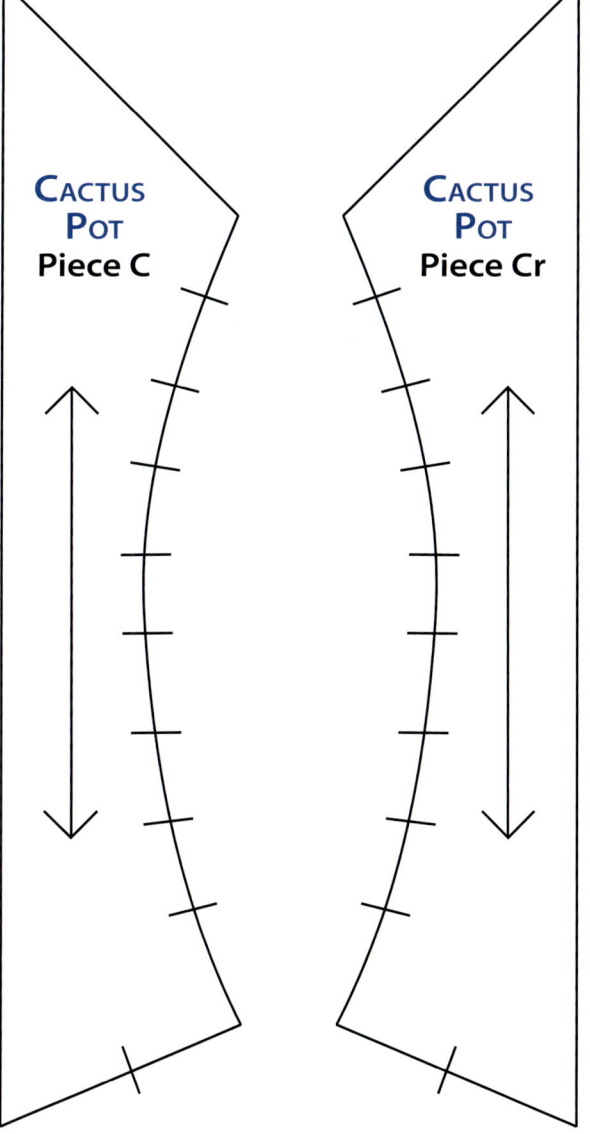

CACTUS POT **Piece C**

CACTUS POT **Piece Cr**

CACTUS POT VARIATIONS

BLUE CACTUS
24" x 24"

Made by Jackie Tonks from blue, white, and green scraps, this quilt clearly shows it is not necessary to plan your color scheme too far ahead. The dark green setting square and triangles pull the blocks together. For the quilting in the center square, Jackie simply stitched through a tracing of the entire CACTUS POT block.

GOUDA CACTUS
24" x 24"

The colors in this quilt reflect the glowing, deep glaze of "Gouds Plateel," the clay pottery ware produced in the Dutch town of Gouda.

CACTUS POT VARIATIONS

SEA CACTUS
24" x 24"

Join four CACTUS POT blocks to form a square, set on point. Set half blocks with borders to form the corner triangles, and the result is this striking design. The appliquéd motif adds an essential focus to the middle of the quilt.

POT NOODLE

Block Size 9" x 14"

This block was named by my husband, a man who suffers a lot for my "art." After designing and sewing yet another pot block, I took a break and wandered into the living room. There sat Will in his usual pose in front of the TV, hand on the remote control.

"Look," I cried, "here's a new pot but I don't know what to call it." Will did not hesitate or even take his eyes off the screen; his reply was instant and uncannily apt: "POT NOODLE." What would we do without the help and support of our families?

This block consists of two parts: a flower part formed by Section A, and a pot part formed by Section B and pieces C, D, and Dr.

Pot Noodle Variations

14" x 20" by Jackie Tonks

14" x 20" by Jackie Tonks

14" x 20"

Three one-block quilts are shown here with a variety of borders. Notice how different the block looks when romantic florals are used, as in the quilt above made by Jackie Tonks.

Make a copy of pattern pieces by tracing or using a non-distorting photo-copier. Join pattern sections on dashed lines as indicated. Make a full-sized master copy of the entire pattern before tracing pattern pieces onto the dull side of freezer paper.

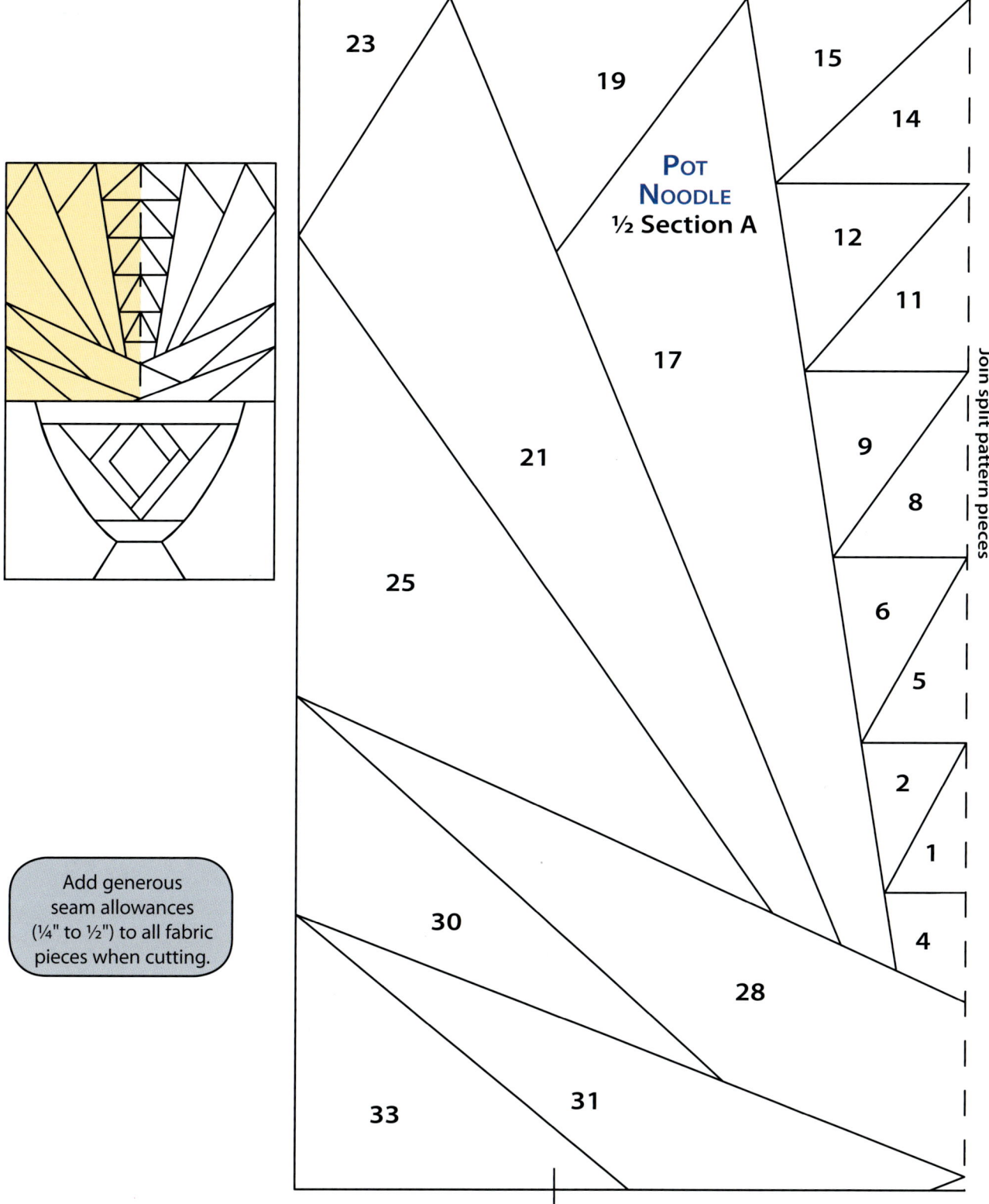

POT NOODLE ½ Section A

Join split pattern pieces

Add generous seam allowances (¼" to ½") to all fabric pieces when cutting.

Add generous seam allowances (¼" to ½") to all fabric pieces when cutting.

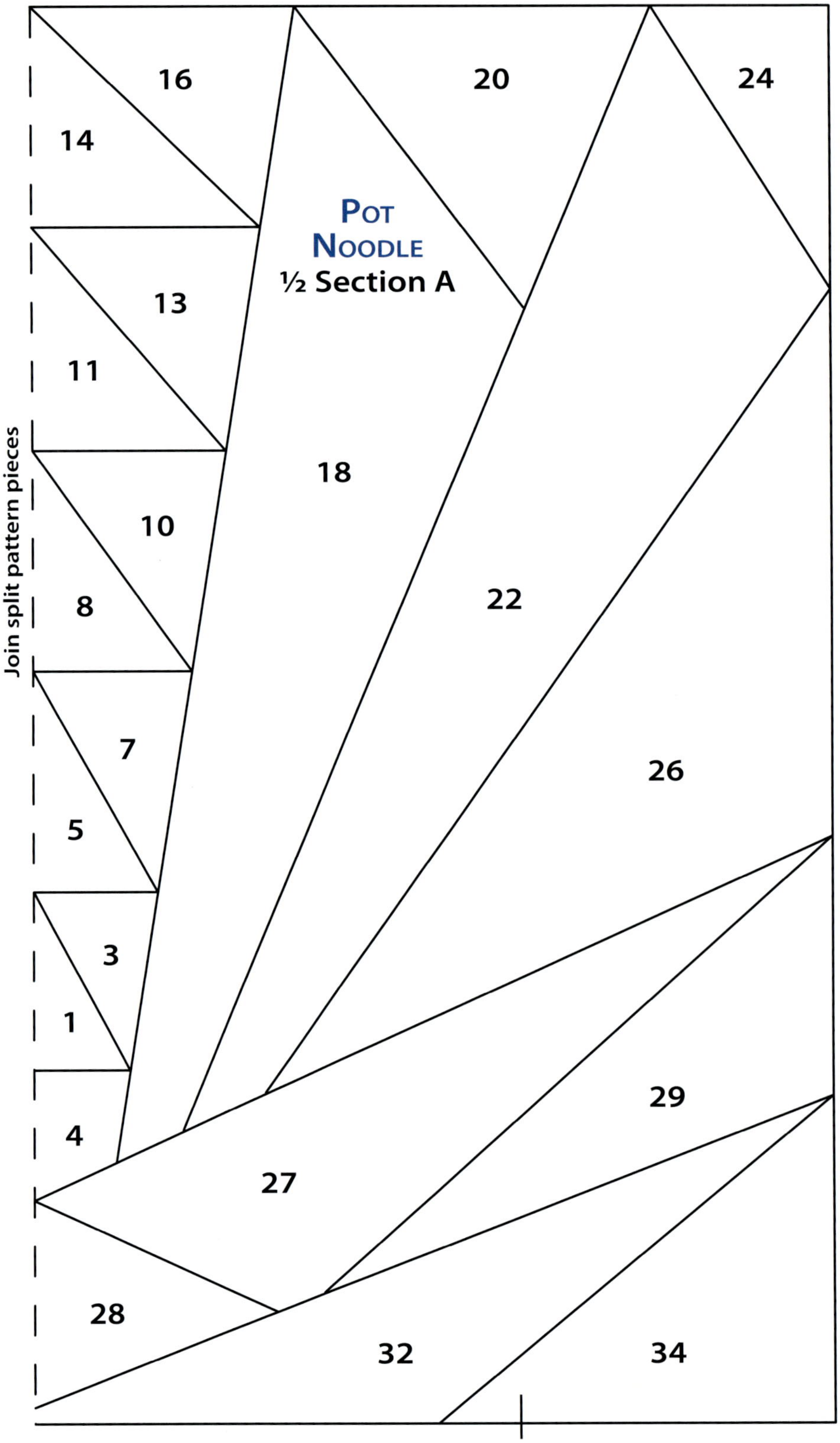

Join split pattern pieces

POT NOODLE ½ Section A

16
14
20
24
13
11
18
10
8
22
7
26
5
3
1
4
29
27
28
32
34

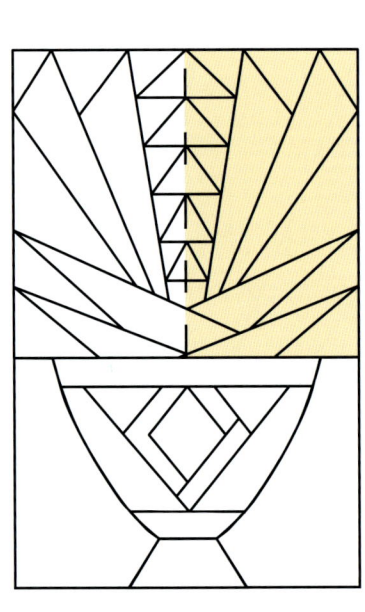

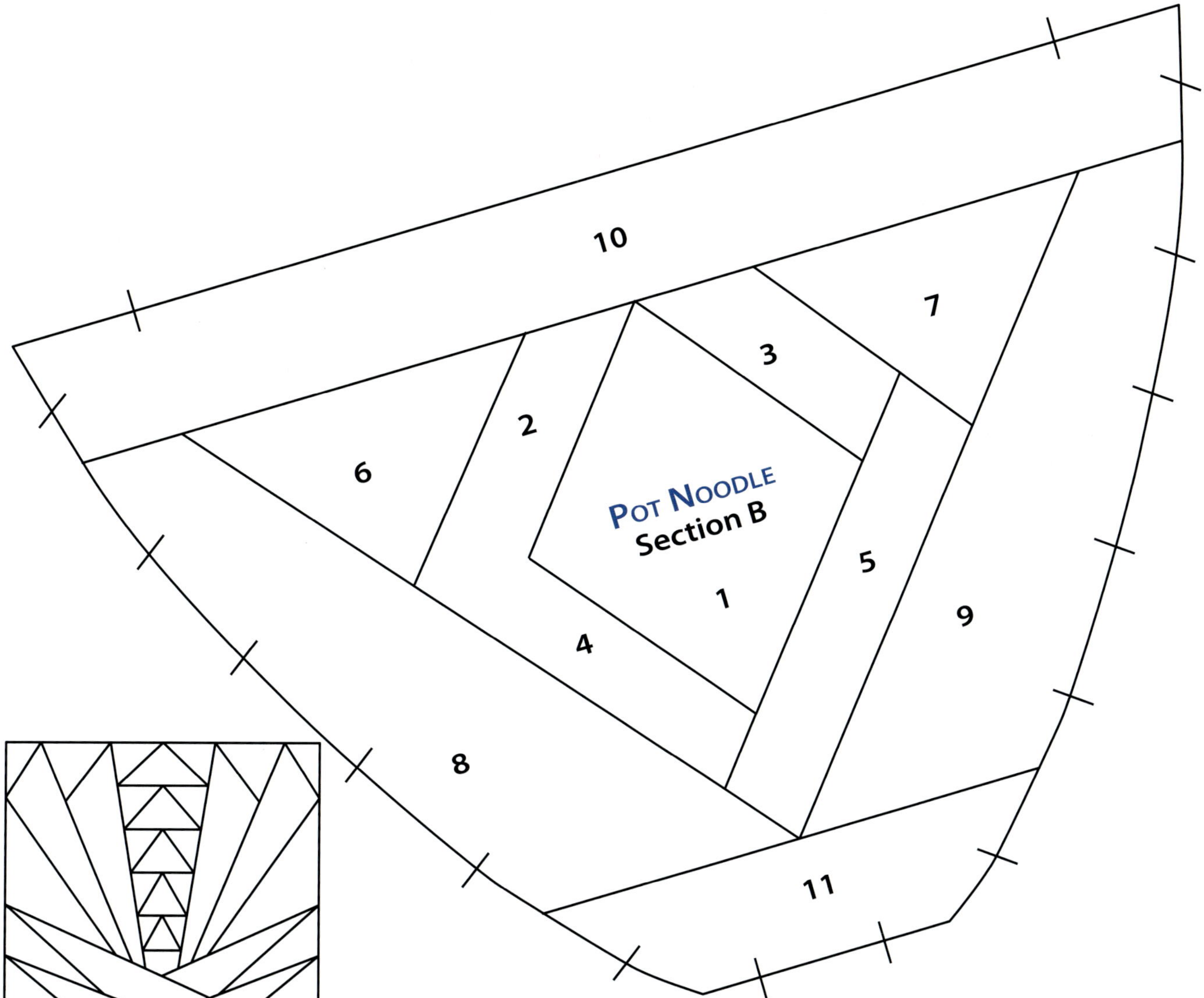

10

7

3

2

POT NOODLE
Section B

6

5

1

9

4

8

11

Assemble the pot section, following the method described in the General Instructions. Join the flower section to the pot section, matching marks.

POT NOODLE
Color Selection

Section A			Section B		
Piece	**Color**		**Piece**	**Color**	
2, 3, 4, 6, 7, 9, 10, 12, 13, 15, 16, 19, 20, 23, 24, 25, 26, 29, 30, 33, 34	Yellow		1	Orange	
1, 5, 8, 11, 14	Orange		2, 3, 4, 5, 10, 11	Black/white stripe	
17, 18	Black/white stripe		6, 7, 8, 9, C	Black	
21, 22	Black		D, Dr	Yellow	
27, 28	Bright green				
31, 32	Dark green				

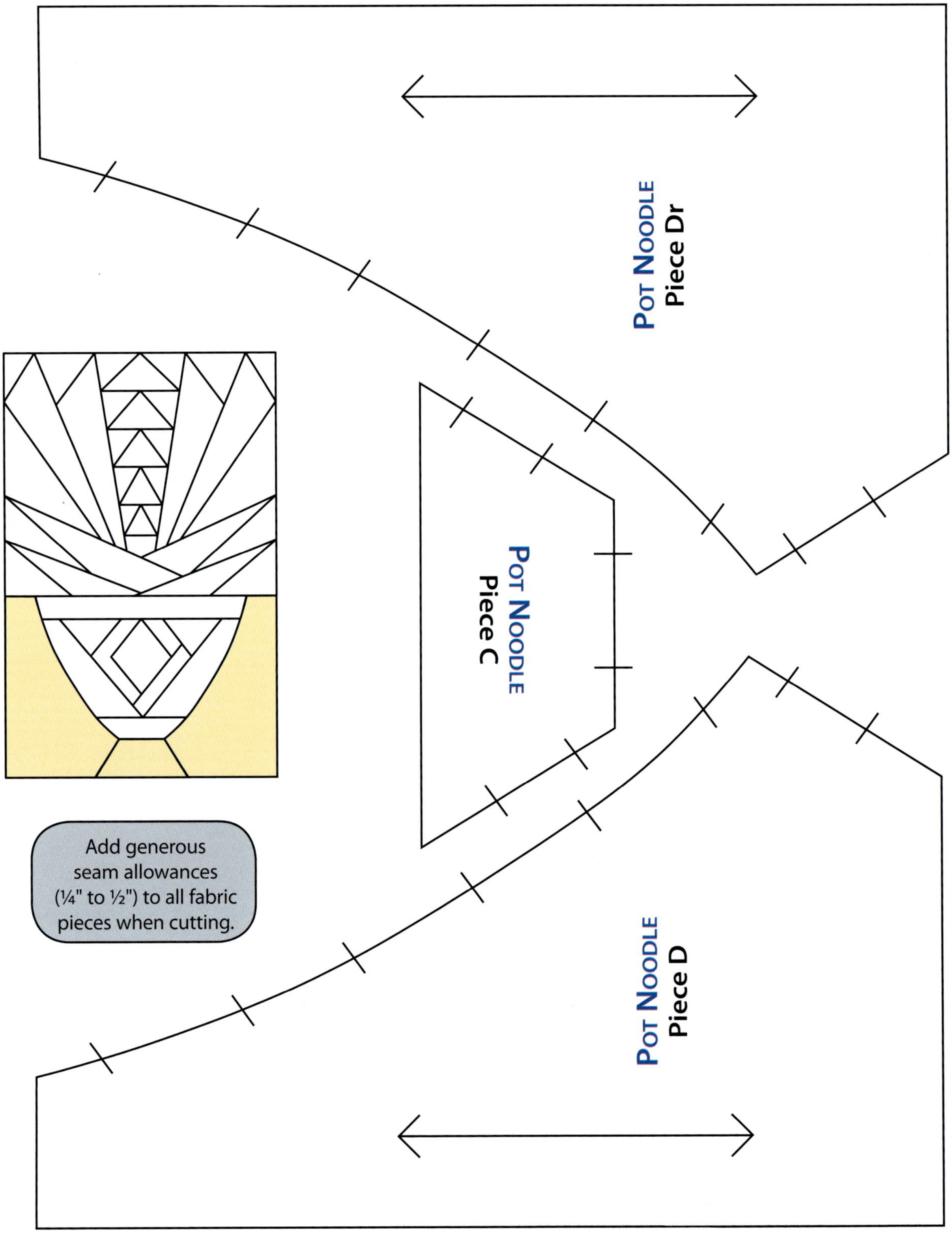

POT NOODLE

POT NOODLE
Piece Dr

POT NOODLE
Piece C

Add generous
seam allowances
(¼" to ½") to all fabric
pieces when cutting.

POT NOODLE
Piece D

TROPICAL HOTPOTS 32" x 17"

POT NOODLE is included in this small wallhanging made with batik fabrics. When using striking fabrics like these, you need only select a few for maximum impact.

FRESCO POTS 36" x 20"

The colors in this quilt are reminiscent of the fresco paintings seen on walls in Mediterranean countries. Compare this quilt with TROPICAL HOTPOTS to see the enormous difference the choice of fabric can have on a design.

More AQS Books

This is only a small selection of the books available from the American Quilter's Society. AQS books are known worldwide for timely topics, clear writing, beautiful color photos, and accurate illustrations and patterns. The following books are available from your local bookseller, quilt shop, or public library.

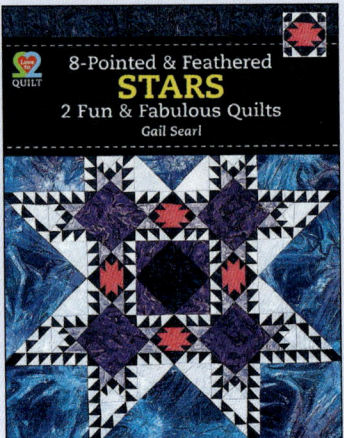

#1284

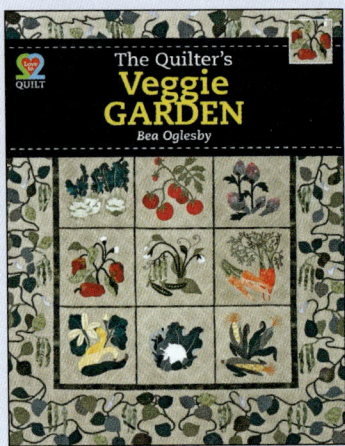

#1287

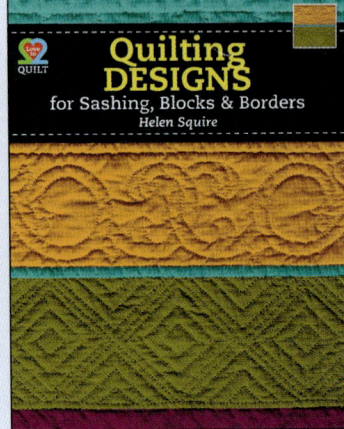

#1286

#1292

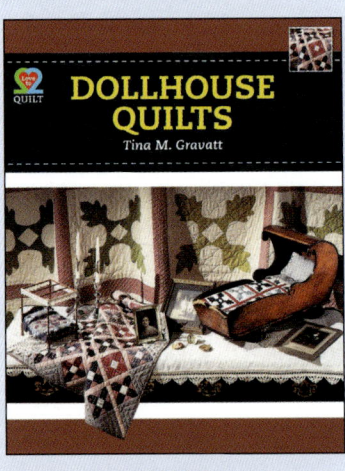

#1290

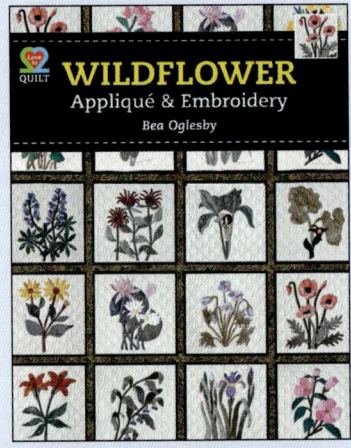

#1289

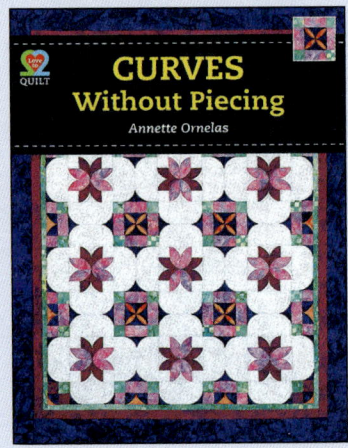

#1293

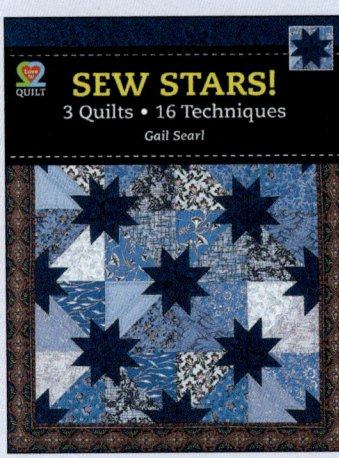

#1295

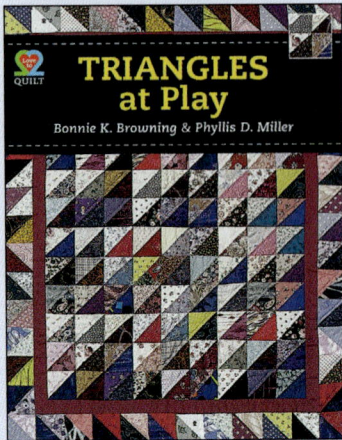

#1297